LIFE IN LOCKDOWN

WRITTEN BY **KELLY FARRINGTON**
ILLUSTRATED **BY TIM WELLS**

Life in Lockdown – First Edition

First published in 2020
by Farrington Consultancy Ltd,
trading as **KellyWellyBooks.**

Farrington Consultancy Ltd
is a private company.

Registered office:
35 Stamford New Road,
Altrincham, Cheshire,
WA14 1EB

A CIP catalogue of this book is
available from the British Library.

ISBN 978-1-8380661-0-9
(Paperback)

ISBN 978-1-8380661-1-6 (MOBI)

Interior Layout & Cover Design
by Collette Sadler

Cover image by Tim Wells

Edited by Fiction Feedback

Printed and bound by Ingram Spark

KellyWellyBooks

CONTENTS

PUBLISHER'S FOREWORD

Before you start reading **Life in Lockdown**, it is important to understand that it is dealing with delicate subject matter. At the time of printing, the virus has infected over 10 million worldwide and killed a reported 500,000 people.

The authors take this crisis very seriously. They have friends and family working in the health sector, as well as vulnerable family members. The illustration of a nurse in PPE in this book is drawn from a photo of a niece at work. Thus, neither author intends the book to make light of coronavirus or offend anyone. Particularly not those who have lost loved ones to the disease or are struggling with its economic fallout.

Life in Lockdown came to fruition by accident, as two creative people furloughed in their respective homes needed an outlet for their energies. The authors have tried to approach the subject sensitively and with compassion. If you think you will be offended, or struggle with the material, then please avoid reading it.

In Britain we are blessed with a unique sense of humour. The coronavirus crisis has seen 'dark humour' come to the fore. It is how we deal with death and disaster in this fantastic country of ours and the book reflects that characteristic!

The fact COVID-19 is personified as a cartoon character is a device to support the narrative of lockdown. The coronavirus is not offered as the hero of the piece. Not at all.

It is hoped that, at the very least, the book will stimulate discussion about the consequences of coronavirus.

YOU STARTED IT!
NO! YOU STARTED IT!
WELLY
2020

HELLO FROM THE AUTHORS

Life in Lockdown is a collaboration between two good friends, Kelly Farrington and Tim Wells. Having been furloughed from our respective workplaces, we suddenly had time on our hands.

With close family members working in the NHS, Tim created artwork centred around the corona theme. This inspired Kelly to write poems to accompany the images, and the idea of a book was born.

The collection of pictures and poetry outlines what it is like living in 2020 Britain during the unprecedented 'lockdown'. Reflecting the seriousness of the coronavirus attack, but also illustrating the gallows humour we Brits share.

To think, this all started with a viral mutation from bats in a far-off province of China. Or did it start with pangolins? Neither of us had even heard of pangolins before the pandemic.

In the future we shall be able to tell those too young to remember, or yet unborn, that there was a moment in time when the planet

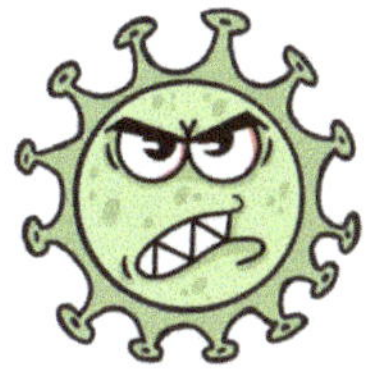

stopped. When Governments halted flights and we all had to stay at home. When, every week, communities stood and clapped the valiant NHS. We learned new words like 'furlough' and 'PPE'. The motorways were devoid of traffic and the air was clean and fresh during our one daily exercise.

At the time of writing the pandemic is still ongoing, but this first edition allows readers to capture their own thoughts, good or bad, on the final pages. Informative, whimsical, and thought-provoking at times, it is a book to keep and look back at in years to come.

Carefully selected charities whose donations have been hit hard by lockdown will profit from our efforts, as reflected by the sales of our book.

We hope you enjoy,

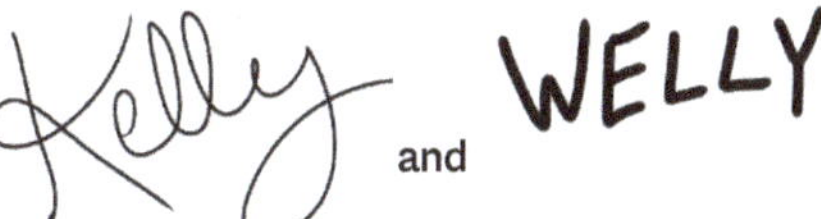

HOW IT ALL STARTED

On 27 December 2019, Dr Zhang Jixian, head of the respiratory department at Hubei Provincial Hospital, reported to health officials in China that a form of novel coronavirus was behind a number of deaths in the region.

It was not until the 5 January 2020 that the World Health Organisation (WHO) published its first Disease Outbreak News on the virus, COVID-19; thus formally revealing it to the world.

On the 31 January two Chinese nationals staying in a hotel in York, one of whom studied at the University of York, became the first confirmed cases of COVID-19 in the UK.

The true horror of corona entered the national consciousness during February and early March. Disturbing news of high infection rates and deaths in Italy, then Spain, reached Britain. Images of bodies in wards and corridors made main evening news broadcasts. A modern Italian health service struggling to cope under the pressure of high infection rates served as a warning to the UK.

By the 27 February, the total number of confirmed UK cases was reported as 16.

Yet, despite the news from abroad, daily life continued as normal.

The first UK death of a person testing positive for COVID-19 occurred on the 28 February.

On the 11 March, WHO declared the virus a pandemic. Reports suggested that the virus had mutated in a Chinese 'wet market', allowing it to jump from bats to people. This evaluation has since been questioned and until Chinese authorities trace 'patient zero', it is not proven.

The question mark over the source of the virus has since been complicated by US President Donald Trump and conspiracy theorists suggesting that the Chinese invented the virus in a laboratory.

Cases started to rise sharply in the UK from mid-March, with deaths tracking a few days behind. Amid a flurry of sporting cancellations, it seems incredible now that the Cheltenham Festival was allowed to commence on 13 March.

On 23 March, the nation held its breath as UK Prime Minister Boris Johnson made a keynote TV address. In an unprecedented step to attempt to limit the spread of coronavirus, the UK was put into lockdown. Nothing would be the same again.

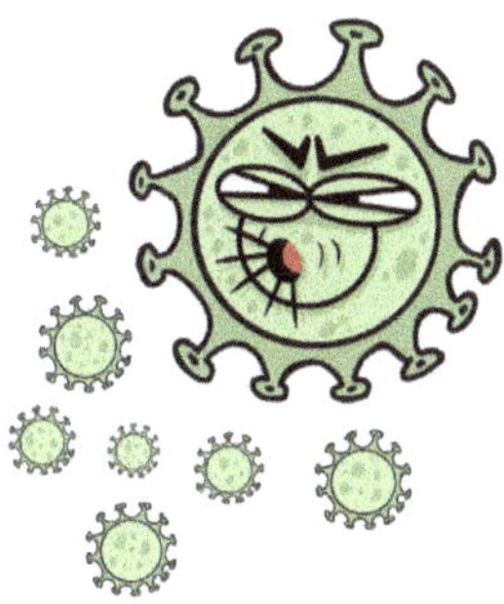

CORONA

I am the stealthy virus silently stalking.
The shadowy exhalation's unseen strike.
I am the pulsating ooze, fecklessly uninvited,
Leaping across to the blink of an eye.

In a dank distant market I mutated,
Among the cages and plastic tanks.
In fetid lab's black din I saw animals
Piled high, like the spell list of an angry witch.

Some packed in tub's congealing swell,
Many on lives' sweltering last gasps hanging.
Other fights lost to death's shrunken filmed eyes.
All at careless folly's convenience displayed.

Species existing since close to Creation,
But, by your demands facing plated extinction.
In vendor's profit, their agonised destiny cemented,
Subjugated to digestive tracts' acidic ending.
Now, opportunity my hosts' suffering spawned,
Given putrid chance to re-emerge transformed.
In ignorance cultivated, but sloppily set free,
I am Man's new immortal enemy, steeped in irony.

With the speed and agility of a winged hawk's swoop,
Whooping with delight, I made good my escape.
From harsh regime's deportation I explored
By other means my global transmission's plan.

10,000 feet up, to all four corners dispersed,
Or aboard gigantic tins on oceans floating,
Where people crammed of their own choosing.
Fast moved I, where fortune's proximity allowed.

Satiating my desire to devour, with viral fangs
Striking the unwary: millions in quick succession
I infected. Yet you mock me still by your light count,
Failing to measure the nature of my testing flight.

My methods and origins are well understood,
Scrutinised under microscope, slides politician's glaring
Denial at being warned: threat's inaction magnified,
As my other incarnations gave fair chance to prepare.

This one with complexity added by Her to heed:
A few unusual twists to ignore innocence
But target those whose consumptive waste expands
The relentless hunting of crimeless animals to feed on.

For I am the agent under Mother Nature's command,
Issued in Her exasperation at being ignored.
Making time tick remorselessly against those with none,
The next Armageddon boxed, but will She keep the lid on...

LOCKDOWN

On 23 March 2020, the UK was put into lockdown. By then many people were aware of the threat posed by the virus, with some already choosing to work from home.

The new Chancellor, Rishi Sunak, announced measures to support businesses having to close down during the crisis. The measures involved grants to some industries hardest hit (like hospitality), Government-backed loans and the opportunity to 'furlough' staff. The Government was to contribute 80 per cent of furloughed monthly salaries, up to a monthly ceiling of £2,500.

The elderly and those with underlying health conditions were proving particularly susceptible to COVID-19. The Government recommended that these groups stayed isolated with no physical interaction between people from other households.

One of the early consequences of news about coronavirus was that many essential items were stockpiled. Despite pleas for people to stay calm, milk, pasta, rice, bread, soap and toilet rolls disappeared off supermarket shelves.

ODE TO THE STOCKPILING TWITS

It's piled to the ceiling, I won't give you the key.
Loo rolls and pasta, flour and some tea.
Eggs, jam and honey, beer and yet more
Beer to fill 'Spoons, it's flowing out the door.

I won't drink Corona. I hope you won't too?
It must be real dodgy and give you the flu!
I'm a world expert on Covid, I've read all the posts,
I wash all my food and head to the coast.
I like family picnics and can't see the harm
Of parking in lanes and strolling 'cross farms.

It came not from bats. It was invented in labs,
A Chinese plot. (And you can get it from cats!)
So be in no doubt that I know the lot,
I'm the stockpiling twit who gives not a jot.

Ridiculous now, a few weeks have passed,
Since I filled up my trolley, and struggled up the path,
With twelve plastic bags, but no room in the fridge.
I filled up the garage, but then came the hitch.
I'd bought too much fresh stuff, had to chuck half it out,
I'm the stockpiling twit who behaved like a lout.

I emptied the shelves and took it all home,
Now I'm knee-deep in loo rolls, my neighbours all moan.
So what, they missed out on all those supplies,
I'm hiding my stash and won't be chastised.
You can say what you want, rules apply to others,
I'm outspoken on social, my profile's a cover.

To do as I say, and not what I do.
And believe what I say, my posts are all true.
Laws are just daft, put there to flout,
I'm selfish and heartless, I complain and I shout,
I load up the car, meet friends and go out,
I never catch colds, I'm bombproof no doubt.

I'm the stockpiling twit, who just caught a bout...

The notion of 'social distancing' entered the British vernacular, although 'physical distancing' was a less popular term preferred in some media. The inference was that limiting social interaction could be damaging to mental health.

While daily exercise was encouraged, the Government recommended people maintain a 2-metre gap between themselves and those from outside their household at all times.

Coughing, a sign of contagion, became socially unacceptable in public.

Schools were closed, except for the children of 'essential workers'. Essential workers included our doctors, nurses, health visitors, and those responsible for public safety or emergency services. Food stores, delivery drivers, public transport workers and utilities all fell under this banner.

The hospitality industry, including pubs and restaurants, closed overnight. All non-essential shops also closed. Unless businesses could operate from home, they found themselves struggling to survive and furloughing staff. Even those operating from home saw work dry up and had to furlough employees. Many companies entered a state of hibernation.

Unfortunately the Government overlooked those who had moved jobs in February. They were not entitled to be furloughed by new employers and were left in limbo, as were directors of small limited companies who paid themselves through dividends. The Government refused to cover any part of those payments, so many small business owners were left struggling and having to take out loans to survive.

With the gym closed, I told
you we would find use for our
stockpiled pasta and rice.

Families stayed at home, often separated from elderly parents who were considered to be at risk. For many the situation caused fear and anxiety. As shops quickly sold out of masks, we started seeing people wearing home-made versions to shield themselves from infection. Even sanitary towels and bras were being touted as unlikely alternatives to cover faces!

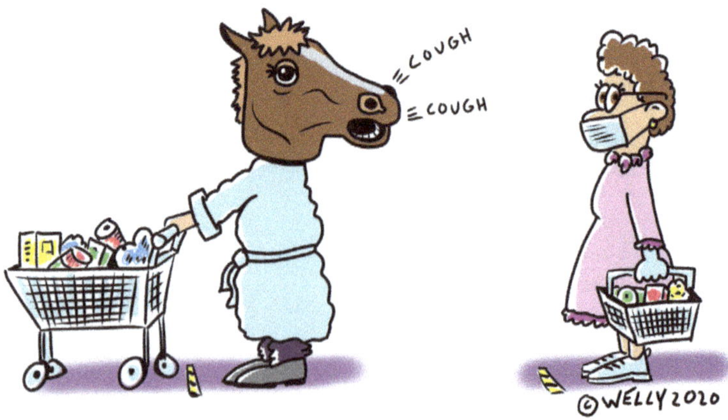

Sorry, I'm feeling a bit hoarse...

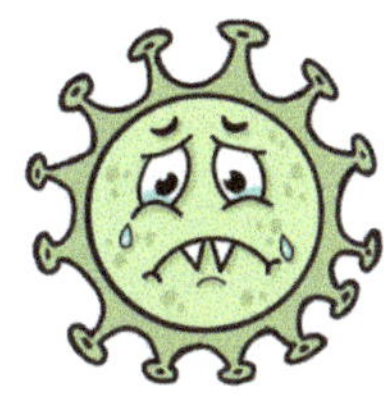

The need to protect the vulnerable separated families across Britain. But many in relationships found that to obey Government guidelines they had to conduct those relationships at a distance. Warnings about depression and mental health were touched on by the media, as suicide rates reportedly increased.

Care homes and retirement homes had to lock down tightly, preventing the relatives of residents entering buildings. The Government came under fire for allowing residents who had been in hospital to return to care homes. Multiple deaths in care homes around the country were attributed to residents infected with coronavirus being allowed to return to their homes from hospitals, without first being tested or going into quarantine.

MISSING MY LOVE

Sunny out, I strolled to town,
    Exercise to escape lockdown.
Turning into lonely street,
    Drawn to the café where we would meet.
Coffees both and cake to share,
    Me drowning in your brown-eyed stare.
Our table's empty
    And my heart is too:
Life's not the same
    If I can't see you.

I asked you to come,
    You argued against it.
I know you are right
    And don't find it offensive.
It's a drive for you,
    And the police might ask why
You're alone far from home.
    It's not worth the try.
It was wrong to suggest, I admit.
    You live with your mum,
A chance to transmit,
    The idea was dumb.

She was in hospital last year,
      Now locked in your flat,
Endless TV and stroking the cat.
      A little old lady, living in fear,
You as her carer,
      So far, yet so near.

The long lonely days all
      Morph into weeks,
Feeding the pain
      My loneliness seeks.
Routine lost to self-pity,
      Depression takes hold.
Weary and jobless,
      My service unsold.
My clients don't need me
      They are closed too,
I used to have many
      But now I have few.
I'm scared what comes next,
      If I'll find work,
Paying rent with no money,
      Where this virus will lurk.

It seemed exciting at first,
    Now it is boring.
I'm missing My Love,
    Hence this outpouring.
You are my star,
    You turn me around,
Make me feel good,
    Pick my chin off the ground.
So I wait for our moments,
    The ones shared on Zoom,
Bringing your sunshine
    Into my room.
Separation's ache,
    My stomach churning,
Missing your kiss,
    And the touch I am yearning.
Until such time comes
    I know I must wait,
Hoping to end
    The solitude I hate.

*Mary believed her husband was
taking social distancing too far.*

Many people working in essential industries, such as the NHS, chose to stay away from families, rather than risk returning to the home carrying corona. With shortages of Personal Protective Equipment (PPE), health centres and care homes resorted to sourcing their own stock.

Hospitals and medical centres were sent home-made PPE from generous local businesses and volunteers who turned their skills to making the equipment. A community spirit prevailed as people realised that the NHS needed more than just a weekly clap to boost them.

It was clear from the early days of the pandemic that health workers of all kinds were putting themselves at risk through their work. Some people saw nurses as the new front-line soldiers in the war against an invisible enemy. Many nurses, however, preferred not to use that analogy. They quietly got on with their jobs of giving patients the best chance of recovery.

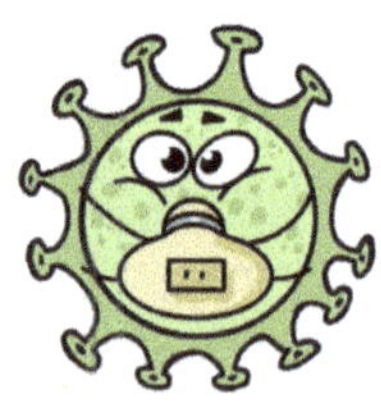

With pubs, restaurants, sports and recreation venues closed, home entertainment took off. In an attempt to alleviate boredom, ever resourceful Brits found new ways to exercise and amuse themselves. Jigsaws, old board games, home baking and quiz nights gained popularity. Products such as yeast and flour began to sell out in supermarkets.

Pandemic, the new game for all ages. Play it inside for fun, or outside for real …

Business video conferencing
software became widely used to
keep in touch with loved ones and
to join in with quizzes.

*Dave took lockdown
quiz nights very
seriously.*

Jokes emerged about the fact dogs
were getting more exercise than they
ever did before lockdown, as family
members would take it in turns for
a long walk with their family pet.

*If I hear the word
'walkies' again...*

At the same time that many dogs were getting fitter, the rest of the nation was eating and drinking too much and putting on weight. We saw stories of elite athletes struggling to train and using creative ways to stay fit. The 2020 Olympics in Japan had been put back to 2021 and all other major sporting events, like football's Euro 2020, were cancelled.

CONFUSION SAYS 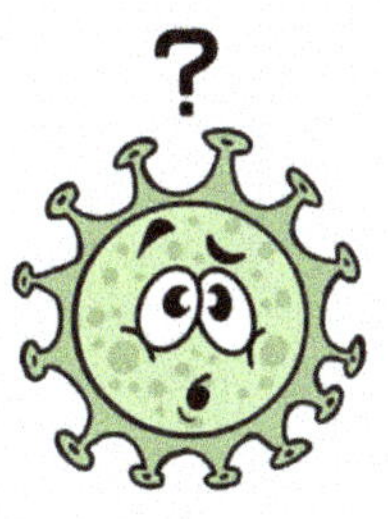

As the killer stalks the streets
Take comfort in our TV screens
Daily instructions what to do
If you know what's good for you
Stay inside if you can
Kill the virus by washing hands
Go out once to exercise
But stay close to home
And try not to drive
Any further than you can walk
Making sure you don't stop to talk
Yet do go out to buy your food
Socially distance when you queue
Work from home unless you can't
And if you must, catch a bus
Avoid public transport
Maybe wear a mask
Although that might be
More dangerous
Covid can kill us all
So follow the rules

Listen
They are very easy
So don't look confused
Obey them and do not flout
They will change soon
And you can all
Go out!

STRESSED PET

O please no, not another one,
Says the dog to itself as you prepare for a run,
I've been out already and it's hot in the sun,
Your wife took me out, your daughter, your son!

So lace up your Nikes and run by yourself,
But before you do, put my lead on the shelf.

My paws are so sore from the pavements we pound,
So stop treating me like some working class hound,
I'm better than this; I'm not made to flog,
I'm your only star pet. I'm your favourite dog!

And when we go out it's all very strange,
It's quiet and eerie; nothing's the same,
And when we see people, nobody stops,
They used to stroke me outside of the shops,
Have I stopped looking the cute little whelp?
It gives me anxiety, I'm needing some help.

I must be a Bad Dog,
What have I done wrong?
Now people avoid me,
Have my puppy looks gone?

They move to one side,
Like they're scared of me now,
But I've bitten no one; not even growled,
I'm adorably cute, of that I'm proud,
I went to puppy school and know what's allowed.

And back in the house it seems even stranger
My master runs to the window when there's no danger
The milkman, the postie, the binmen, Ocado...
He looks really sad and says he's on furlough,
I do not know what he means by that word,
It's a new one on me, one I've not ever heard.

But it's my job you see: to jump up and bark
O no, here he is, we're off to the park!

WELLY ©

THE PLANET WAKES

Soft shines the light
Where neon once blazed bright
The empty streets delight
At lockdown's peaceful sight

Quiet tarmac where death was fated
Little creatures infiltrated
Gardens, parks and the precinct
Not seen for decades, thought extinct

While up in the sky
Fuelled jets flew high
The birds no longer care
Singing brightly, they own the air

Raptors follow the chain of food
On garden fence, completely new
Astonished pics on social posting
'Look what I've seen!' they're boasting

Deer wander through central Nara
Wild boar romp in Barcelona
Mountain goats play in Llandudno
Vancouver's inlet sees orcas on show

Elephants, monkeys, wild cats and swans
More seen on flags, national icons
Alligators, snakes and many bears
Concreted habitat that once was theirs

Looking to horizon's return
Worse will come if we do not learn
Reminding us all that we are fleeting
As if they know, as if they've seen

In hospital buildings everywhere
People dying, people scared
The virus slowly filling lungs
Choking, clogging fibril sponge

The irony we know too well
A story that is hard to tell
That as in us the virus seethes
The planet wakes and starts to breathe

THE NHS

The seriousness of the virus cannot be overstated. It was an indiscriminate killer, and ICUs throughout the country soon began to fill. The Government took the step of setting up additional 'Nightingale' hospitals in several major towns and cities, including 4,000 beds in the ExCel, London.

In a remarkable twist of fate, the Prime Minister, Boris Johnson, contracted the illness. He was kept in an ICU and his life was saved due to the care he received under the NHS.

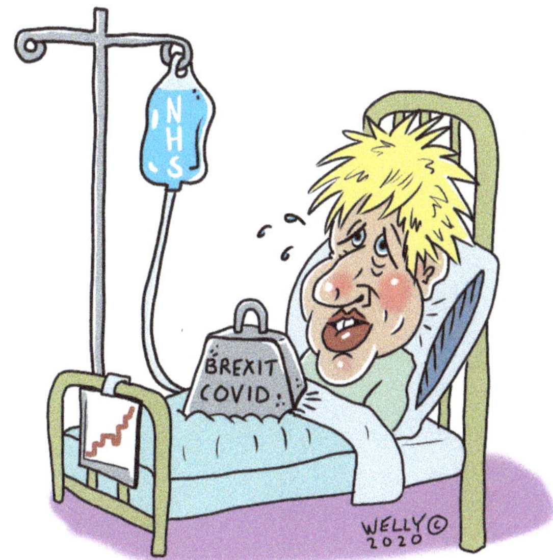

Stories and footage emerged about the conditions within ICUs and about NHS staff performing heroics to save others. Putting their lives at risk, often with inadequate or uncomfortable Personal Protection Equipment hurting their faces, they performed their tasks.

Many health professionals died, contracting the virus while in the line of duty.

As the total number of deaths steadily mounted, the suffering of patients in ICUs was harrowing news on daily TV bulletins. By early May, the number of certified corona deaths in the UK was second only to the USA. The total number of deaths jumped from around 20,000 to over 30,000 as the Government started to include care home deaths in the total.

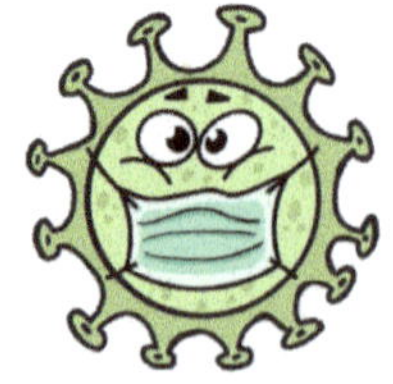

JOURNEY INTO THE INFERNO

Oft do I glance at the ward's outer gate,

As we struggle in sweat amid Viral Gore.

Hoping and praying, yet still they bring more.

Divinely comedic lined up in blue masks,

In furnace's face, adhere our tasks.

Resolute we stare down Danger's exigent eyes,

Imp's foaming mucus, choking a patient.

'Help,' sighs thorax path, blocked off zephyr

To the fiery lungs filled with Its Legions.

Therefore, I think not to judge when I test.

That they sinned or not; nor I to question

The how and why, which lives led best.

Seeing Human beauty in her various forms,

And if they adored not God so what?

For who says they are the ones to be scorned?

The machinery counts the lives in its timing,

Bleeps' deep green peaks; lines are defining

The precarious way they cherish this space.

Spirit within, fought Death and some triumphed.

Driving the Thing back to Hell,

To appear again in someone as infected swell.

Hunting down the Foe's Familiar returning.
    It's you again, doing the choking and burning.
    Pushing me harder and near to wit's end.
On the seventh night of nine I stumbled,
    Amongst the wretched, the Beast held me.
    Placing my fear before me.
For they lay face down in Desperation's rows,
    Throats punctured, hanging on by a thread,
    Cries fading to infinity, I could see no end.
And in that dark shadow of perdition,
    As standing at the crater over Suffering's lava,
    Hope I saw not. Only Misery beguiled in mine own
Face swelling welts, stung by Grief's tears,
    Reflections unrecognised in exhaustion.
    Trying to sleep but mind's rest distortion.
'Twas last week amid blood and carnage I fell.
    'Rise up,' the Doctor said, 'Defeat banished here,
    You shall not meet that Charlatan today.'
My eyes lifted to see, amongst the ward beds,
    Lucifer had left me, elsewhere to prey,
    Chance I took to repose, and reset.
Back to the shift in battle ground's visor
    To Shield, and the Lancet weapon, Advisor.
    Sage Medics' humble vistas beside us.

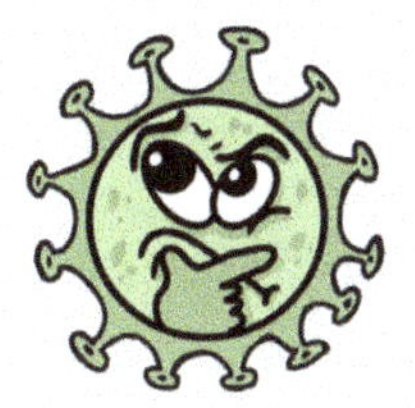

Blocking out fear's din drowned by our hymns,

    And as if in answer a miracle was struck,

    93 he was, fallen comrade rising up.

Jubilation's comfort in the Human condition,

    Guard of Honour applauding and singing,

    To see Hope's eternal light rekindled,

Energy forged for the Fiend's onward fight.

    Amongst the tumult a resolve we found,

    And reinforced from outside these fort's walls.

It came to pass we faced the Villain down.

    Stood proud but not Heroes,

    'This is what we do!' we say.

As once again, I C U on a trolley come in.

    'We know you well now,' smiles I,

    'So let our new battles begin.'

I shy not, choosing to behold your eyes,

    Till when we rejoice and can say this is over,

    In vaccine's victorious injective puncture.

Convulsed the time Monster's wounded to die,

    And scarred, I will return to this brightened world.

    On glorious day, but what have we learned?

Banished, patiently strains new await,

    Mutation the Minion called to infiltrate.

    Chancer to come back even stronger?

To meet Mankind's fate, held up in the stars.

HEROES EMERGED
NHS STAFF

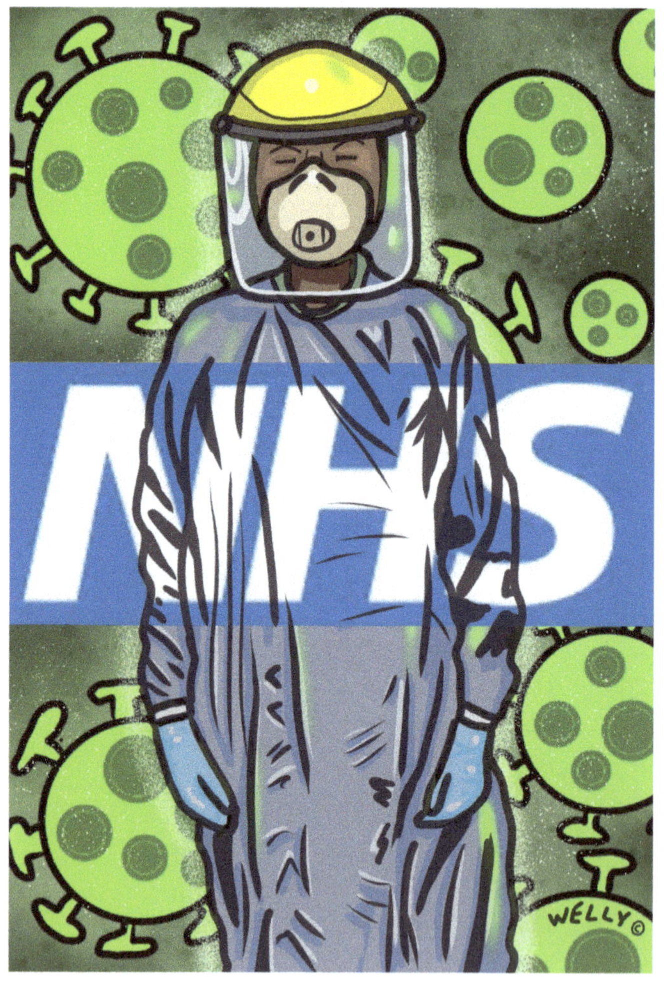

TOM MOORE

99-year-old ex-World War II veteran Tom Moore single-handedly raised £33 million to support the NHS. A truly astonishing effort. The Captain's 100th birthday was marked with an honorary promotion to Colonel. Shortly afterwards Tom Moore was knighted, becoming Sir Tom Moore.

RAINBOWS

All over Britain painted rainbows magically appeared in windows, on walls, roads and on banners in gardens. The rainbows acted as a symbol of hope in support of the NHS.

RAINBOW

Red Danger's alarm

Orange Health   under threat

Yellow Deceitful   virus unleashed

Green breathes   the Environment

Blue Calming NHS   uniforms of faith

Indigo Spirituality but   no dignity in death

Violet Mother Earth   breathing new life

X MARKS THE KILLER'S SPOT

Cold viral fingers   expertly exploring

Finding a way to   stop zephyr's exhalation

Delights in your   struggle instead expelling

To the point of   self-asphyxiating

Expectorating, goo is   in mucus, inside of you

Produced from the mucous membrane

(So don't get them mixed   up, the virus never would)

Tenacious and mucopurulent   in its haemoptysis

The expectoration of   blood from the lungs

Thick, viscous mucus, sputum   or mucopurulent sputum

Choking the unfortunate;   condemning, the desperate

drowning

in

their

own

dripping

secretions

THE BRIGHTER SIDE

BRITISH HUMOUR

During the lockdown, British humour came to the fore, a means of counteracting the desperate daily COVID-19 related news. Home schooling, drinking too much and putting on weight were all subjects of the nation's social media discussion.

Parents expressed their appreciation of teachers, after seeing their own teaching standards slipping following a few weeks of tiring home-schooling.

FOOTBALL

Football fans all over the country missed watching their teams either live or on TV. Discussions ensued about how it would be possible to re-start the football season safely.

In mid-May the German Bundesliga restarted, with games being played to empty stadiums. The sterility of playing matches with no atmosphere did not excite the majority of British fans.

The Scottish Football League voted to end the season, declaring Celtic as Champions. The English Premier League, however, re-started the season on Wednesday 17 June. It seemed the break affected goal line technology, as Sheffield United saw a clear goal not given against Aston Villa during their 0-0 draw.

*It's time they relaxed the
social distancing rules.*

FURLOUGH EXTENDED

Although some industries went back to work, on 12 May the Government announced an extension of the furlough scheme for a further 4 months.

*I've just been furloughed
to prevent a spike.*

VE DAY 75TH ANNIVERSARY CELEBRATIONS

On 8 May Britain celebrated Victory in Europe Day. Bunting appeared as street parties were held up and down the country. Unlike previous anniversaries, there were no tables in streets, as social distancing meant that neighbours had to celebrate within their front gardens.

For the second time during the crisis, the Queen appeared on TV to address the nation.

Is it Christmas already?

Physical distancing at a street party...

LOCKDOWN HAIR

Lockdown hair, designed to scare
Affecting the furloughed everywhere
Taking the bedhead to higher levels
Never has Britain looked so dishevelled

Stripes of grey glinting in the sun
Impossible to fix, access to salons gone
Trying block colours from a supermarket shelf
There's no cure for the outcome
Not even the National Health!

Looking like a scarecrow
Frightening off birds
Our hair's never looked this bad
And we've never smelt worse

And with the hair a new dress code to match
A suitable canvas for the untidy thatch
Grubby dressing gowns in need of a wash
As embarrassing as a public cough
Long and straggly, you dare not answer the door
Now your hair's been put up into a pompadour
Where you used to be shingling
You're the walking dead minging
And instead of the selfies
You're reposting the memories
Of a Facebook time you once looked fab
Before the Government enforced Corona Drab

The only consolation you have is this
All your mates cannot take the diss
Knowing they face mirror shocks too
Because they look as bad as you!

EXITING LOCKDOWN?

On Sunday 10 May a recovered Boris Johnson addressed the nation again on TV. In his address, Boris outlined a tentative three-stage lockdown exit plan to get Britain back to normal within three months.

The Government's slogan, 'Stay at Home, Protect the NHS, Save Lives' changed to 'Stay Alert, Control the Virus, Save Lives'. While Boris made it clear lockdown was not ending, a new 'Alert' app was launched to echo the message. The Government also planned to use the app to track and trace the spread of the virus.

The app did not work properly and was dropped on 18 June.

Boris set out which sectors of the economy could return to work, as long as distancing safety measures were put into place. People could also exercise more than once a day including playing sport within their family groups.

The following day the Government published new guidelines, giving the detail many people were asking for. To prevent a double spike, any further relaxation to rules would be conditional on the 'R rate' (the average rate one person spreads the infection) equalling less than 1.0. Should the R rate increase, the Government said they would curtail any relaxation of lockdown to prevent a second spike.

As many headed back to work, alterations to travel arrangements, office configurations and physical interactions had to be examined and overhauled. For each work situation, there was a new set of guidelines to follow. Many people returned to work with a degree of trepidation, not knowing within whom the viral killer lurked.

On Sunday 17 May there was some encouraging news from Alok Sharma, the Business Secretary. He announced that clinical trials at the University of Oxford were progressing well and, if successful, some form of COVID-19 vaccine could be ready by September.

The Government aimed to have 30 million vaccine doses available in September and promised a further £84 million of funding to accelerate research at Oxford and Imperial College.

But the Government went onto caution that an effective coronavirus vaccine may never be found.

On 18 June the Government announced that they had started manufacturing the vaccine in advance of clinical trial results. Some commentators in the media reported that the Government's approach suggested that trials were going well and likely to succeed.

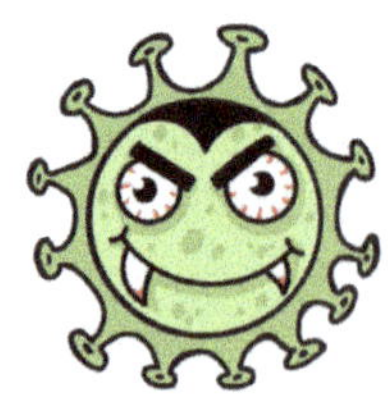

Before I can do the survey Mrs Addams, has anyone in your household had COVID-19?

BARNARD CASTLE EYE TEST

Then on 22 May news emerged that Boris Johnson's chief advisor Dominic Cummings had driven his family to Durham while infected with corona.

The clamour for Cummings to resign obscured good news that the UK's daily infection rate had been decreasing since mid-May. Although deaths were now approaching 40,000, the daily rate of deaths was also decreasing.

Encouraged by the decreasing infection rates, Boris Johnson announced dates for more sectors returning to work, including fashion retailers.

By defending Dominic Cummings, however, the Government seemed to be contradicting their own legal guidelines, adding to the general confusion felt by the public. Labour leader Sir Keir Starmer said Boris Johnson's decision to take no action against Dominic Cummings was 'an insult to sacrifices made by the British people.'

The controversy surrounding Dominic Cummings's trip to Durham and his excuse that he'd driven to Barnard Castle on his wife's birthday as an 'eye-test' rumbled on for over a week, as did the apparent confusion surrounding some of the Government's public advice.

Meanwhile, over the pond in the USA, President Trump came under fire for spending time on the golf course on the day American deaths registered as being caused by corona passed the 100,000 mark.

Kimblesworth
riston
Witton
A167
Pity
Me
amwellgate
oor
West
Rainto
A690
Wear
2
62
Carville
Litt
Gilesgate
Moor
5
Sl
She
DURHAM
New
cepeth
A18
Langley Mo
Brand
JELLY Shincliffe
2026
4
A177
10
A1(M)
Sunderland
Bowbur

The New York Times

VOL. CLXIX ... No. 58,703   NEW YORK, SUNDAY, MAY 24, 2020

U.S. DEATHS NEAR 100,000, AN INCALCULABLE LOSS

They Were Not Simply Names on a List. They Were Us.

Numbers alone cannot possibly measure the impact of the coronavirus in America, whether it is the number of patients treated, jobs interrupted or lives cut short. As the country nears a grim milestone of 100,000 deaths attributed to the virus, The New York Times scoured obituaries and death notices of the victims. The 1,000 people here reflect just 1 percent of the toll. None were mere numbers.

STAY AT HOME
DON'T STAY AT HOME
DON'T GO TO WORK
GO TO WORK
WELLY
2020
STAY SAFE
DON'T STAY SAFE
DON'T WEAR A MASK
WEAR A MASK

#BLACKLIVESMATTER

On 25 May, Minneapolis police received a call from a convenience store employee claiming a man had bought cigarettes using a counterfeit $20 bill. Police arrived and arrested George Floyd, a 46-year-old black man.

With a knee to his neck and head against the concrete, George Floyd pleaded with officers, repeatedly saying, 'I can't breathe.' Only seventeen minutes after the first squad car arrived at the scene, George Floyd was dead.

Upon his death, George Floyd became the face of one of the largest uprisings in modern American history.

Over the next few days anger grew as video footage of Mr Floyd's death spread globally. Demonstrations took place across the planet. In the USA, UK and Australia, statues of historic figures were targeted. They were deemed by protesters to be symbols of black oppression.

Huge crowds gathered in many UK cities, ignoring Covid restrictions. Significant numbers of protesters clashed with police in London. Twenty-seven, officers were injured in the worst week of violence up until 8 June, dividing public opinion on the nature of the protests. The protests had reportedly been hijacked by those with other political agendas who wanted to provoke violence. There was also a fear that the large crowds would re-ignite the spread of corona.

For many, however, the death of George Floyd galvanised opinion that we need a fairer and more equal society; one in which the colour of our skin no longer matters. Despite the danger of large crowds spreading corona, most protesters' demands for societal change was (and still is) well-intentioned.

At the time of writing, these protests are ongoing.

RIP George Floyd, 1973-2020. #BLM

GEORGE FLOYD

George Floyd
Gentle giant
Resurrected
An issue we can't avoid
13th Amendment 1865
Slavery abolished
And freedom promised
Yet two centuries on
Under the knee of the law
Blacks still die
Habeas corpus scorned
Finally will the penny drop?
Black Lives Matter
Racism must stop!

WHAT NEXT?

Whatever happens, it looks like there will still be stormy waters ahead for Boris Johnson as his Government attempts to exit lockdown whilst avoiding a double spike of infections. The game-changer will be rigorous UK-wide anti-body testing to establish those who have already been infected and hence may have strong immunity to the virus.

Not knowing how long any immunity will last does mean that an effective vaccine is needed to bring an end to the crisis. Otherwise the virus will always remain with us and become globally endemic, rather than a pandemic!

Did anyone tell the local wildlife?

POST 2020 VISION

And finally, how will people look back at this remarkable era?

Will it lead to a fairer society: one within which the true value of essential workers is acknowledged and rewarded? Will Governments look to restrict the likelihood of new viruses arising by banning wet markets and the globalised mass production and transportation of food? Will Governments understand and build on the return of nature and environmental benefits created during global lockdown? Will anything fundamentally change?

Maybe it is too soon to ask. Until a vaccine is invented and life returns to normal, it is difficult to predict the longer term repercussions of Covid. The final poem of the book is about how the pandemic may appear to an alien class observing Earth from a faraway universe. The class is given some interesting homework…

AN ALIEN'S 2020 VISION

Good new moon class, open your books,
An interesting one we have, let's take a look.
All settle down and calm your blue skin,
Quiet at the back, let me begin...

On a small ball of lava, land, gas, and water,
Curious bipeds evolved amid slaughter.
Life was tough, so they lived in small tribes,
They did what they could to get on and survive.
They cherished the elders, looked after the weak,
As they evolved, they learnt how to speak,
Artfully crafting, their stories in song,
Intelligent reason: they knew right from wrong.
One bright spark harnessed heat's fire,
Now at the apex, taking all they desired.
Farming came next and that went so well,
That over millennia their numbers did swell.
Breathing rainforests were slashed and then burned,
Connections with nature recklessly spurned.

The industrial age, dark smog's shiny new era,
In the blink of an eye; from wood, coal to nuclear.
People and nations, led not by the wise,
Wars and genocide: lands colonised.
The insidious advance of the corporate machine,
Idolising 'profit' and wealth most obscene.
Carbon emissions warming the globe,
Oxygen depleted, no trees left to grow.
Polluting the air over plastic-choked seas,
Melting the ice caps with crude mining debris.

The intelligence once to nurture and care,
Senses dulled by a flat hand-held stare,
Chatting far more, but communicating less,
Understanding lost in cyber-stress.
Grabbing all desired, no thought to the waste,
Worshipping celebs with no style or taste.
Coveting the objects displayed on a screen,
No thought of true value, or production's means.
Exploiting, in factories enslaving the poor,
Pushing them harder to make more and more.
Millions left starving in barren dry lands
Facing extinction, and by their own hands!
So that was their history; it all came to this,
A species called Mankind stood on the abyss.

But what came next might surprise you my class,
In their year 2020 something strange came to pass.
Now turn the page in your galactic texts,
And I shall tell you what happened next...

It started in China, a place known as Wuhan,
Amid wet market's stench an infection began,
With globalisation, the virus did spread,
Pandemic worldwide, many soon dead.
'Stay inside', the people were told,
'The virus is dangerous and killing our old',
As in the past when elders were treasured,
Their leaders issued protective measures.
Around the world, known as 'lockdown',
The streets became quiet in city and town.
Cars did not move and planes left on ground,
Animals flourished as freedom was found.

Then came a pause to consumer pressure,
Pollution decreased, the air became fresher.
People were allowed daily exercise,
Noticing nature and birds in the skies.
At home they baked and used their food wisely,
Caring for neighbours and acting more kindly.
Valued those doing work so essential,
In previous times viewed as inconsequential.
Through a digital haze no longer sleepwalking,
Treasuring the time with grandparents talking.
Live face-to-face, family and friends re-connected,
Schools closed, but learning new skills unexpected.
Wearing the same clothes day after day,
Expensive labels forgotten: all tucked away.
With time to reflect on what matters most,
Ending their greed, placing values foremost.

That concludes my class for today,
What are the lessons to take away?
The planet I describe is a lot like our own,
So carefully consider what I have shown.

Ah, so you ask, 'What happened next?'
That's a good question; I'll give you context.
That was not history, that's up to date,
So your homework will be to predict their fate.
Under the title '2020 Vision',
Write an essay about what you envision.
On the brink of extinction, is Mankind doomed,
To die of greed, and in suffering entombed?
I leave it with you, and give you the scope,
To write if you think those beings have hope...

Before we go home, did
you wash your hands?

YOUR CORONA DIARY

We hope you enjoyed **Life in Lockdown**. Keep this book to look back at this extraordinary time. The final pages are dedicated to your experiences of the pandemic. Write them down here to refer to in the future.

Will a vaccine be invented to
defeat the virus, or is this to be
continued...

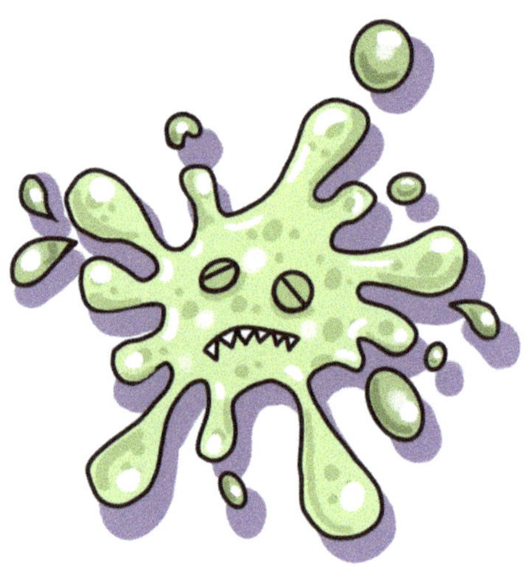